How to Find
your Best Job Ever

How to Find your Best Job Ever

Maggie Neilson
CGA, MBA, CPC

About the Author

Maggie Neilson is a Certified General Accountant, with a Master of Business Administration degree. Maggie is also a Certified Professional Coach. She has over 20 years of senior executive experience overseeing finance, human resources and information technology departments in entrepreneurial environments. In her multi-faceted career she has held the positions of Vice-President Marketing, Chief Financial Officer, Chief Operating Officer, and Chief Executive Officer in various industries, including real estate development, manufacturing, film and printing. She excels at leading corporations through periods of challenge, such as high growth, re-organizations, sales and mergers.

Maggie has learned the value of highly-engaged employees and high-performing teams in leading companies through uncertain times. She is the President of Executive Decisions (www.executivedecisions.ca), a professional coaching practice focused on assisting people to advance their careers with purpose and passion. Maggie has written this book to help you find your best job ever – a job that matches your passion and purpose, and is in alignment with your values and personality.

Maggie Neilson
MBA, CGA, CPC
604-306-6604

Executive Decisions
edcoach@telus.net
www.executivedecisions.ca

TABLE OF CONTENTS

It's Time to take Control and Find your Best Job Ever

Have you ever started a new job only to find that you have a bad feeling in your stomach on the first day? It all sounded so good in the interviews, but now that you've arrived something just doesn't feel right.

It's like the joke about the woman who dies and goes to heaven, only to find out that all her friends and family went to hell. As much as heaven was a wonderful place she became very lonely. She asked Saint Peter if she might be able to visit hell to see if her friends were okay. The Devil was notified and permission was granted for a one-day visit.

When she arrived in hell she was quite surprised. While heaven was serene and quiet, hell was bustling with music and laughter, bars and restaurants and everyone seemed to be having fun. She had a wonderful time and found it hard to leave.

For the next few days she reflected on her experience and how much she missed her friends and family. She decided to approach Saint Peter and ask for permission to return to hell permanently. Imagine her surprise on returning to hell and it was, well ... Hell ... fire, brimstone, misery. In her dismay she turned to the Devil and asked what happened to all the parties and good times?

The Devil replied, "That's when we were recruiting you – now you're ours!"

Once you've been recruited, you may find that you are in such a bad job that you have to take another bad job just to escape!

Let's face it, there are a lot of bad jobs out there. Most of us have had jobs where the culture is sick, the business practices are unethical, chances for advancement are few and far between, pay increases are hard fought, and your manager is a bully. Okay, the chances of all this going wrong in one job are slim, but we all have had some of these things happen more than once in our careers.

Working consumes at least one-third of your day, and if it is a bad experience it may affect the other two-thirds as well. Daily experiences at work also affect personal and family relationships. All this means that we should give the same amount of thought to a job selection as we do to picking a friend or a spouse.

Unfortunately, many of us leave all of the decision-making up to the companies: it's no wonder we are often disappointed after we finally land a new job!

This book contains solid, practical advice to help you take control of your career and find a job that matches your values; to take control of the interview process and help you find your best job ever.

I've been both an employer and job candidate many times in my career, so I can tell you what happens on both sides of the desk. By taking control of the hiring process and finding your best job you will reduce your stress, live your values and achieve more job satisfaction.

All of the experiences I've shared in this book are true stories. I've changed the names to protect people's privacy.

THE BENEFITS OF GOOD JOBS

Whether we like it or not, work is central to most of our lives. Jobs give us financial security and personal identity, and may even allow us to make a meaningful contribution to our society. Workplaces also provide us with a social identity – we often define ourselves by what we do for a living. Our jobs allow us to create a structured life, with social interactions, regular routines, team membership and purpose. Employers are slowly coming to realize that their employees' health and well-being impact their productivity.

TRUST AND RESPECT COME WITH GOOD JOBS

Respect is central to the creation of positive workplaces. Respect is due regard and does not require there be a personal relationship. Respect can be relatively easy to maintain in a professional setting. However to truly engage employees, trust must also be present.

Trust is the firm belief in the reliability, truth and ability of another. Trust may exist even where there has been no investigation to support the belief. For example: we often take people at their word. When our bosses trust us this increases our sense of value to the organization and our pride in ourselves.

There are numerous demonstrations of respect in the workplace:

- Employees are invited to contribute their **opinions** to decisions that impact them. This can be as simple, such as having individual choice of their office chair, or more complex, such as managing the overall design of the workspace.
- Employers take steps to ensure **pay rates** are equitable. This does not mean that wages are necessarily the highest in the market, but that the rates have been set considering the competition, location, and other relevant factors. No one appreciates being underpaid.
- The work place is **safe and secure**.
- Employees are given opportunities to **improve their skills**. This can be as simple as "lunch and learn" sessions, formal team building or sharing tuition costs for higher education.
- The workplace does not tolerate **incivility**.

   Workplace incivility is characterized by low-intensity behaviors that violate respectful workplace norms. Uncivil behaviors are characteristically rude and discourteous, displaying a lack of regard for others. Incivility is distinct from violence. Examples of workplace incivility include insulting comments, denigration of the target's work, spreading false rumors, and social isolation.

Demonstrations of trust sometimes are more personally satisfying:

- Job sharing is becoming more common and requires

5

trust from co-workers and from management.
- Companies that allow telecommuting are making a very positive statement of trust.
- Use of company credit cards implies trust in employees' decision-making.
- Trust can be demonstrated by both employee and employer being flexible and accommodating in addressing the needs of each other.

Dave was an airline employee facing retirement who had long wished to start his own small business. His employer had no restrictive policies against this, but Dave never seemed to find the time he needed. He approached his supervisor with a plan to rearrange his weekly work schedule so that he could work four ten-hour days, instead of five eight-hour days. His supervisor agreed to a trial run. Dave found that he enjoyed his shifts more because he felt more in control of his schedule, which improved his morale and increased his energy. Dave's experience was so successful that others in his department have varied their hours as well. This flexibility resulted in a far happier and more productive team. Best of all, he did start his own business and it was a success. He retired from his job a year later.

If trust was not present in the organization this proposal would never have been considered. The supervisor was trusted to make scheduling decisions, and Dave was trusted by his supervisor to complete the extra hours. Dave was also shown respect by his supervisor. The company would not be affected if he created a small business. However, by being flexible the company increased Dave's loyalty, which he modeled to his co-workers until the day he retired. The company's demonstration of trust in Dave helped foster a culture of mutual trust.

Why are Trust and Respect Important?

One word: **Engagement**. We all know the difference in our work habits when we are bored, unmotivated, and disengaged. Not to mention when we are downright angry. No one goes the extra mile for anyone.

However, when we feel truly valued we become engaged: we complete our tasks with enthusiasm and attention.

THE PROBLEM WITH BAD JOBS (WHAT BAD JOBS DO TO YOU)

Have you ever started worrying about Monday morning on Sunday afternoon? Do you wake up in the night thinking about your job? Do you notice your heart beating faster, or a feeling of dread in your stomach as you approach your workplace? Are you taking more sick days than before? These could be signs of being in a bad job.

With today's hectic pace, we are all operating under a higher level of stress than before. We are expected to keep up with the speed of information, and keep pace with technology. All of this creates stress, and when we think of stress, most of us think of these kinds of job-related stressors.

However, relationships at work are just as important when

it comes to stress. When relationships are dysfunctional we enter a whole new world of stress. Think of what happens when we are treated rudely by a customer, a supervisor or colleague. We stew, rerun the conversation over and over in our heads, and complain to friends. We certainly aren't concentrating on our job.

Over time, incivility can damage key working relationships. What happens when people cannot get along, yet their co-operation is necessary to complete their work? It's very painful for them and all the people around them.

Problems caused by Stress

We all know that stress, especially unremitting stress, can cause a multitude of problems such as:

- Sleep deprivation
- Digestive problems
- Headaches
- Depression
- Anxiety
- Hypertension
- Heart disease
- Substance abuse
- Eating disorders
- Relationship and family problems
- Loss of concentration
- Poor memory

Human Resource professionals are noticing that more and more people are taking disability leave due to stress-related problems. People are simply burning out, becoming unable to continue in their jobs. It has been observed that in previous times people would work until they collapsed with heart attacks. Nowadays, with relatively healthier lifestyles, many people work until they collapse with emotional illnesses such as depression.

Many of us have taken control of our diets and our exercise, but have neglected to take control of our careers.

Productivity can also start to suffer when negativity creeps in. Most employers will quickly notice when this happens and address it with meetings and/or progressive disciplinary actions. Not only is this unpleasant, but it creates a trail of events that may follow you to future positions.

> Remember, bad news always travels faster than good.

Even those who manage to hang on in unfulfilling jobs may attract unwelcome attention from their employers. Unrelenting stress can affect all aspects of our health, resulting in more illness and absenteeism. If there is one thing a supervisor notices, it is sick time. More and more companies limit the amount of annual sick time available, and may start to dock your vacation pay or force you to take unpaid leave. A friend of mine learned this lesson the hard way.

> Jennifer was a union employee at a major airline. She had been with the company for over twenty years in many different positions. As a result of the reorganization of the company she had to choose between two positions. One had lesser seniority doing a job she liked at the airport. This meant that she might not get the prime

shift times she wanted. The other job was in a call centre, but she would have greater seniority and be able to hold the more desired shift times. She hated telephone work, but she had worked very hard for her seniority. What a dilemma! Unfortunately, she chose the call centre position. Very soon she found that she hated every day on the job, and it became increasingly difficult to force herself to go to work. She started calling in sick more and more often, and eventually was calling in more than three days a week. This had disastrous consequences on her personal and professional life. Not only was she formally reprimanded, but she lost her prime time shifts and had her hours reduced. She eventually was forced to refinance her home. Even worse, Jennifer actually did start to feel depressed as she focused on all the negatives of her job. This eventually resulted in the end of her marriage.

Due to the absenteeism issues on her file she was targeted by her manager as a problem employee. Without the support of her supervisor or her union representative, she didn't take the necessary steps to arrange a medical leave. Unable to take the time necessary to heal, she eventually had no option but to accept early retirement.

While it is not legal for an employer to dismiss you or fire you if you are medically unable to work, it is not uncommon for people to ignore the signs of severe stress. When these conditions start to impact your work, your employer can start progressive discipline procedures which may lead to dismissal or lay off. The onus is on you, not your employer, to initiate a medical leave by meeting with your doctor.

Is it Time to Move On?

Signs that it's Time to Move On

Even people with great jobs have off days. So a few bad days should not cause you to start firing off resumes. However, if any of the following issues keeps recurring, it may be time to change.

- It's not about the money. Raises or bonuses are just not giving you that sense of satisfaction you once had.
- Futility sets in. It feels as if nothing you do makes a difference. If you feel that way, just hope your boss doesn't figure it out before you find yourself a better alternative.
- You aren't learning anything new. The job has become routine and you've explored all possibilities to add new responsibilities or projects. There is little or no opportunity for education.
- You aren't being encouraged. No one is speaking to you about future opportunities.
- You hate your supervisor. Try to get out … before your supervisor figures it out.
- You keep feeling that workplace activities are in conflict with your values: who you are and what you stand for are at odds with your job.
- You don't have any friends at work. There is nothing

worse than being disconnected socially with your team.

- Your boss is callous about your time: he or she expects you to be available 24/7, or sets unreasonable deadlines and then ignores the project when it is delivered,

If several of the above apply, it is likely that it is time to move on. I have reached this decision point more than once in my career.

At one time I was trying to decide whether to accept an offer from a new company or stay with the job I had been in for almost ten years. This was a real dilemma for me because I loved the company I was with, its people and products. I had helped it weather many crises. My judgement was clouded by emotion and passion, so I turned to my husband for advice.

Imagine my surprise when he pointed out that I dealt with unremitting stress every day, was paid less than my male colleagues in similar positions, and recently had received little or no recognition for the extremely positive results I had achieved. This lack of recognition was causing me to work harder to achieve more noticeable results. However, the bottom line was there was nothing I could do to win approval. I had to realize that I had gone as far as I was going to go in this company. This was a tough love moment. I resigned immediately and accepted the new offer.

The harder I tried the less I received in return. How could I have missed all this? Remember the old story about how to boil a frog? If you throw the frog into a pot of boiling water, it will immediately jump out. However, if you put the frog into a pan of luke-warm water and slowly heat it to a boil, the frog will relax and cook before it knows what is happening. I was a cooked frog.

I believe the problem with abusive jobs is that they are like bad relationships: they usually start out in a positive place and then move slowly, inch by inch towards toxicity. It starts slowly with a few criticisms, and then perhaps a less than favorable performance evaluation. Maybe you are passed over for advancement, or someone else takes credit or is given credit for your work. All of this can slowly erode your self-confidence and motivation, creating a vicious cycle.

Abusive jobs are an extreme example, as my situation was a few years ago. However **there are many degrees of "non-fit."** It might simply be that you do work that is uninteresting and unrewarding, but it's easy and it's a pay cheque, so why rock the boat? While this might be acceptable for some, for most of us it's definitely not.

So why do we stay in these jobs? Are we complacent, fearful or lazy? Like me, are we too busy "doing" to notice how we are being treated? Is the devil we know better than the devil we don't? Whatever the reasons, the bottom line is that we stay in positions that are not aligned with our values, and this can cause us real problems.

However, sometimes things can seem pretty bad, but **choosing to move on would be the wrong choice.**

A few years ago I accepted a lateral move in my company. While I continued to report to the President, my new role brought me into closer contact with her on a daily basis. Although I did not know it at the time, the company was in financial turmoil and about to have their loans called by their bankers. In all my past dealings with the President we had worked well together and had a mutually respectful and professional relationship. However, in this stressful time, we did not work so well together. She was short tempered, demanding and not easily pleased.

I was initially extremely tentative and anxious. However, because I was aware of the President's source of stress I was able to maintain my objectivity and focus on my contributions. My passion for the company and my strong work ethic got me through this difficult time.

Six months later, when the crisis was over, the President's good humor was restored.

The two experiences above share a lot of similarities, but in one case I stayed in my job and the other I moved on. The point is that it's not so easy to recognize when we are in the right or the wrong job.

How to Tell the Difference between a Hopeless Job Situation and a Temporary Problem

Make a start by evaluating your current job. Answer the following questions:

- **If you were offered your job today would you accept it?** Consider this carefully. Is your current negative feeling temporary or permanent? Are there some changes that could be made that would increase your satisfaction?
- **Do you like the company you work for?** Are you proud to be associated with your employer?
- **What would you be giving up** if you left the organization? Do you have years of service that entitle you to extra vacation or leave allowances, pension benefits or other benefits that would take you years to build again? And if so, are these important enough to you to be worth putting up with unhappiness?

Remember that even good companies can go through periods of negativity and stress. It is the firm's reaction that makes all the difference. Here are some ways that positive workplaces can alleviate fatigue and burnout.

- Providing encouragement and expressing gratitude: this can go a long way to alleviate stress and fatigue. A few kind words go a long way, but make sure that they are genuine and honest. If your supervisor is simply repeating the same speech over and over, your stress could actually increase.
- Recognizing efforts: this can be achieved through words of praise, or offering a reward or small bonus. The rewards do not have to be big, but they will be

appreciated. Rewards do not have to be for individuals; a team can be rewarded. Again the reward should be genuine.

Some employers use rewards to reach specific goals. This is a contest, not a reward.

- Removing barriers wherever possible: a supervisor who understands where the roadblocks are and takes steps to remove them is showing their staff her or his staff they are heard and valued. These efforts are not always successful, but by acknowledging that they exist the supervisor is showing loyalty to the team.
- Building some positives into the workday: good supervisors make sure that there is some fun time in each day. Shared positive experiences will strengthen the team.
- Providing recovery time: a good supervisor will be sensitive to the team and provide recovery time for workers dealing with stressful situations. Staff need to debrief in a positive, supported way to recover their energy. Debriefing can be done one to one, or in a team environment.

Rather than ignoring stressful situations, good companies acknowledge them, and counteract with positive support. What do the managers and supervisors at your company do in these circumstances?

ACCEPT THAT IT'S OK TO DIVORCE YOUR JOB

Today, there is no such thing as job security. The average person changes jobs every three to four years. Most of us can expect to have more than six careers in our lives.

This has changed enormously: our parents or grandparents usually only had one career and sometimes worked for just one company for their entire lives. They usually didn't expect to be happy or fulfilled at their jobs: work was, well ... work. However, our parents had benefits that we do not. They usually worked an eight-hour day and left their tools at the office or factory each night. They tended to have more peers, that is, more people doing the same type of work they did and therefore more camaraderie.

These days, most of us are overwhelmed by information, glued to technology and have to be available to our bosses at a moment's notice. More and more jobs are becoming specialized as companies become more streamlined. We encounter more competition with our peers for recognition, advancement and budgets, and due to increased specialization of positions. Overworking is common place: we can in some cases work in relative isolation ... in our slippers ... at midnight. And we have all been affected by downsizing, rightsizing, and outsourcing. (At least in our grandparents' day, they called a spade a spade – you weren't "right-sized," you were just plain "fired!")

The point is, we need to adopt a flexible approach to our careers, and be aware that there will be times when we need to take control of our careers and make changes for our own good.

The trouble is, it can be hard to accept that such a time has come. After all, change is scary for most people.

FACE YOUR FEARS AND START TO MOVE ON

Allowing yourself to become "stuck" is uncomfortable and unrewarding. It can even destroy your health. Everyone has obstacles in their own mind. Try to face your obstacles and follow your dreams.

Once you've decided it's time to move on and you are ready to seek a new position, then you must be disciplined and cautious. You certainly don't want your current employer to know that you are looking.

Consider the following:

- Do you have the time, energy and discipline necessary to complete a job search? Think about your family and outside obligations.
- Have you completed the training necessary to pursue your chosen job? It may be better to stay a little longer if your current employer will reimburse your tuition.
- Don't discuss your job search with anyone at your current place of work.

Once I was considering a staff member for a sales supervisor position. It was a big promotion and I had to spend some time persuading my boss that Jane had the skills and was ready for the challenge. He thought that we should fill the vacancy with an external candidate. It took a number of weeks but I finally prevailed and was able to make the offer. After the dust had settled and Jane was in her new role she confided to me that the promotion was well timed because she had just started to consider looking for a new job. If my boss or I had been aware that Jane was looking for another job we would probably not have considered offering her the new position.

- Read your employment agreement to make sure you understand any restrictions that may prevent you from applying for a position with competitors. You may need to get some legal advice if this is the case.
- Use only private email and voice mails in your search. Office computers are the property of your employer. Aside from that, using office property will send a negative message to potential employers about your integrity and ethics.

Let's assume you're certain that it's time to move on, you've faced your fears and done your preliminary research, so you know there is nothing to stop you moving on. **Now it's time to invest some time in getting to know the most important person in this equation: You.**

STEP 1: EVALUATE YOURSELF

You can't expect to find your best job ever until you know exactly who you are, what you have to offer and what you want. This means that investing time in self-evaluation is a crucial part of the process.

To start, clear your mind of all the previous feedback you have had from friends, family and colleagues. Sometimes our vision of ourselves is clouded by this information, or we have grown and the information is out-dated and no longer fits us. This should be your assessment.

WHO ARE YOU?

Matching your job to who you really are is crucial to job satisfaction. In our jobs we all have seen mismatches and their disastrous effects, such as:

- Supervisors with terrible people skills, who quickly discourage and demotivate their staff.
- Detail-oriented people in strategic positions who become micro-managers and stifle their direct reports.
- Front-line people with little or no customer service abilities.
- Natural leaders who lack positional authority and so cannot benefit the company.

21

The key to finding the right job is to have a clear understanding of who you are and what your competitive advantage is.

We all have a competitive advantage. Each of us has a unique set of values, skills, interests and personal style. You will achieve the highest degree of job satisfaction when these components intersect.

By taking the time to define your competitive advantage, you will be able to make the most of your job hunt by eliminating those companies, industries, and positions where your attributes are neither needed or valued. As you work through the next five sections, write down the answers to each set of questions.

WHAT INTERESTS YOU?

Most of us would start to list our hobbies and sports, but think beyond to those things that ignite your passion and spirit. The questions below will get you started.

I've also provided example answers from a fictional person, who I will call Mike. **The fictional answers are intended to inspire you to dig deep.**

Answer the following questions to establish what your interests are.

- **What do you spend your disposable income on?**

  > **Mike's example answer:** Health products, bicycles, books, techie toys, bike computers, cameras, movies, clothes, entertainment.

- **How do you spend your time outside of work?**

  Mike's example answer: Exercising; cycling;
  walking; swimming; gym; photography;
  gardening; watching movies; spending time with
  wife and kids; watching TV; writing; learning
  new computer programs; learning new things
  in general, such as scuba diving; travelling when
  possible.

- **What is your greatest accomplishment, and why do
  you place such a high value on it?**

  Mike's example answer: Adopting my kids
  and immigrating to Canada. I am proud of
  these accomplishments because both of
  these processes required setting a goal, doing
  enormous amounts of work to make them
  happen, following through doggedly, and finally
  achieving the long-term goal. I place a high value
  on them because both of these accomplishments
  significantly changed several lives for the better,
  including mine.

**Using your answers to these questions, stop and evaluate
yourself.** Sit back and look at your answers, and try to be
objective: **what kind of person emerges** from the answers
you have given?

  As an example: Mike emerges as someone who
  is goal-oriented. He may also be self-motivated

23

Mike's passion will be ignited when he is working for a cause that he truly believes in. He also seems to be someone who would be happiest in a job that gave him sufficient time off to pursue his many interests: a 60-hour work week would most likely kill him. So Mike would need to find his best job ever at a company that valued work-life balance. And of course he needs to find a job where he can utilize his many creative skills.

At this point, you have a pretty good idea of what things and activities you want in life. **As you can see, with a full profile of oneself, it is possible to define quite clearly the kind of job that would make you happy.** Now let's move onto your style, because that's key for getting to the things you want.

WHAT IS YOUR STYLE?

I don't mean your clothing sense. Style is your unique character and where and how you work best. You will most likely be aware of your dominant preferences but, again, think a little deeper.

Answer the following questions to establish what your style is.

- **What is your ideal work environment?**

    Mike's example answer: As little boss-time as possible. I like to do my own thing and set my own priorities. Also, my actual place of work must be reachable by bike or transit, because nothing on earth would make me spend two hours a day in a car. I like to have a window because I hate being cut off from the sun.

- **Describe your everyday working style**

  Mike's example answer: I like to make a list of things to do for the day, prioritize them, get the most important ones done, and hopefully do the others as well. For me, success means I did the vital tasks on deadline. Also, I like to take breaks and move around; I don't like to sit for long periods of time. I like to work collaboratively and try to get people working with me on things.

- **What role do you gravitate towards when working in teams? Follower or leader? Non-participating, or flying beneath the radar?**

  Mike's example answer: I quite like to lead and will do so if possible; but if I am in a team or group where one person grabs the lead and talks all the time, I don't care enough to fight for the leadership, and will just follow that person. On a day-to-day basis, I find leadership a little tiring.

- **Would you rather create processes or follow them?**

  Mike's example answer: I don't have a compelling desire to create processes. As long as the existing processes are sensible, I am happy to work within them.

- **Are you a team player or a lone wolf?**

  Mike's example answer: I love being part of a team and play well with others.

- **Do you like a calm environment, or are roller coasters more your thing?**

  Mike's example answer: Oh hell, I hate roller coasters. Give me a calm life, please.

Let's consider the deductions we made about Mike in the previous section; he's goal oriented, self-motivated and needs to believe in the outcome. **Note how these assumptions are now supported** by his answers to the style questions above. He likes to work with minimal supervision and set his own priorities. He can be a leader, but not just for the sake of leading. We are moving towards being able to develop a comprehensive profile of the kind of job Mike would enjoy.

We are also getting some more information about environment, which will be useful when we start looking at different employers and their locations.

WHAT ARE YOUR SKILLS AND ABILITIES?

Create a list of your skills and abilities. This would include your knowledge acquired through formal education, as well as through training, or informally on the job. Abilities are acquired through experiences at your job, home, or while volunteering.

Here's an example of how to list skills and abilities:

Sue works as a Warehouse Manager for a shoe manufacturer. She obtained her B.A. and pursued a certificate for inventory management from a local technical school (education). She has been trained to use the company's software system, has a forklift operator's certificate, and Level 2 First Aid Certificate (training and skills). She has experience leading teams, scheduling workers, improving process and budgeting (abilities). Sue We might also include some industry specific knowledge based on her product, industry or volunteer experience.

Answer the following questions to establish what your skills and abilities are.

• **What is your formal education?**

> **Mike's example answer**: I have a Master's degree in English

• **What are your skills (what training have you received)?**

> **Mike's example answer**: I have learned desktop publishing and web design.

- **What are your abilities (skills you have obtained by experience)?**

  Mike's example answer: I am a good writer and editor, a good public speaker, can effectively lead teams and work collaboratively.

- **What talents or abilities are you most proud of?**

  Mike's example answer: I'm a great cyclist and a really good swimmer; I write extremely well; I can be witty at times; I am a pretty good public speaker; I'm often really good at following through to achieve goals.

- **What things are you not good at, no matter how hard you try?**

  Mike's example answer: Directions/maps; mechanical things such as repairing bikes; useless at detecting subtleties in people's behavior, e.g. if someone secretly dislikes me, I don't pick up on it. I need people to be open, direct and honest, otherwise I misunderstand them. Useless at responding in the moment when I am verbally attacked in some way, because I'm not a quick thinker – I need time to reflect and digest. I make better decisions when I have time to reflect.

More great information. Note that achieving goals comes up again. Notice that he is most proud of his individual achievements. This doesn't mean that he can't be a team player, but that he works very well on his own. This person cannot read subtleties, so will need to have clear and honest feedback. He will also have to work in an environment where he can take some time to think things through to reach decisions.

Complete a list of your skills and abilities, and then give some consideration to what skills and abilities you really enjoy using, and which ones you don't. Also consider what knowledge you have acquired in recent jobs that you could transition to a new employer.

What are your Values?

Values are our **moral compass**, the foundation of character. If you don't know what you stand for, how will you know when you succeed? No matter how prestigious a position is or how much money you make, you will not be happy if a job forces you to compromise your values. When I speak of compromise I don't mean those little white lies we all tell, or the times that we do what our boss asks us even if we disagree. This goes much deeper. I'm thinking of companies that have unethical products or practices. Think of the recent scandals at TimeWarner and Enron. These examples are pretty extreme, but you get the idea. Your values are based on what is important to you and can be used as your compass to gauge whether you are doing the right things for yourself.

> Having a clear set of values is essential to finding your dream job. Your individual values tell you what it is you wish to accomplish with your life.

29

Answer the following questions to establish what your values are.

- **List one to four people who you admire, and say why.**

   Mike's example answer: my stepson, who
   tackles big projects and gets them done. My wife,
   who has done so well in the business world. My
   daughter, when she works two jobs at a time. My
   other daughter when she is compassionate and
   caring. My grandmother who brought up 11 kids
   on her own.

- **How do you measure your success?**

   Mike's example answer: By asking myself
   questions: Am I happy? Is my wife happy? Is the
   rest of my family happy? Is the dog happy? Do I
   have at least a few friends that love me and want
   to spend time with me? Am I healthy and strong?
   Do I feel like there is some point in getting up
   in the morning? And also by setting goals and
   finishing tasks – e.g. finishing a writing project
   that I have set myself, completing my Masters
   degree. Also by getting pay cheques (salaried or
   otherwise). And by mastering new skills.

- **What are your core beliefs?**

   Mike's example answer: Karma (what goes
   around comes around); life is not pointless
   (there is a plan we just don't know what it is);

there is most likely a God, and so far I have not completely fulfilled everything he or she could reasonably have expected of me, based on what I was given at birth; it is better to be kind and loving than the opposite; as humans we have a responsibility to leave the world better than we found it; family and friends are more important than work (no one on their death bed says I wish I had spent more time at work), so it is vital to find the right balance, but it's not easy

- **How do you want to be remembered?**

    Mike's example answer: I would like to be remembered as kind and loving, and someone who made the world a better place in some way, and someone whose presence is missed because I was fun to have around. When I pass, I would like it to be seen as a little light going out (rather than, "thank God he finally left").

- **What is your chief purpose in life?**

    Mike's example answer: Being healthy and happy, improving myself, learning. Taking care of my loved ones.

Now we can complete the picture of Mike. He is goal-oriented, self-motivated and self-directed. He does not like intense stress. He has a number of abilities and skills to bring to the workplace. His values mean he will be happiest achieving goals he believes in. He will probably do better if he is not in management, and has the chance to use his creative skills.

> **Example Best Job Ever for Mike:** Mike emerges as someone who is goal-oriented. He may also be self-motivated if he believes the goal is worth his time. Mike's passion will be ignited when he is working for a cause that he truly believes in – perhaps an environmental magazine. He also seems to be someone who would be happiest in a job that gave him sufficient time off to pursue his many interests: a 60-hour work week would most likely kill him. So Mike would need to find his best job ever at a company that valued work-life balance. He also would be better off in a company that does not have an extremely hectic pace.

> For example, Mike would not be happy with the roller coaster atmosphere at a local newspaper. And of course he needs to find a job where he can utilize his many creative skills, such as writing and editing. Based on Mike's values, he might be happiest in a job that paid less money but gave him more scope for creativity – management might be possible for him, but it is clearly not important to him, and might serve no purpose except to limit his creative opportunities by causing him to spend time on tiresome administrative duties. Furthermore, the fact that he lacks a certain awareness of subtle emotional

signals might mean that the politics involved in a high profile job would be very difficult for him to manage well. On the other hand, he could be equally happy working independently or as part of a team.

Get a Second Opinion on Your Personal Profile

Creating a personal profile requires self-awareness, as we saw with Mike. However **is this picture of yourself correct?** Are you in denial about certain facts that are obvious to others? For example, everyone uses the phrase "team player," but clearly not all of us are. Many people think they are good at being leaders and are not. A brutal self-evaluation of the latter assumption might entail asking questions such as do people follow me, or do they become sick and quit.

Run your answers by a trusted person, such as a friend or a spouse. See if they agree, or if there's something important you've overlooked.

Lou is an example of what happens when you don't know what you are truly good at and what you are not. Lou was promoted to the position of Sales Manager because he was the highest achieving sales person in his company. He was outgoing, focused, and built strong relationships with his customers. He was competitive and liked to win every sales competition and award offered by the company.

On the surface it might seem logical that Lou was promoted; however he failed quickly in his new position and subsequently left the company – a double whammy. Why did this happen?

As Sales Manager Lou was expected to analyse sales reports, mentor his team, maintain key customer relationships and create company-wide sales strategies. Lou was not an analytical person, so he never read the reports, much less provided feedback to his team. He did, however like to work in the field with his salespeople. This should have been a great opportunity for mentoring but unfortunately Lou highjacked every sales call, taking over the meetings and leaving the sales rep looking weak and foolish. Needless to say, Lou very quickly ran out of support from his boss and his team.

Lou's story highlights the importance of doing what we actually **want** to do, and what we are good at. This notion may spark a wistful thought of roads not travelled. It might even mean that you need to make a longer term plan to achieve your ideal job.

You may wish to consider some formal personality testing and career assessments. This may take some time to achieve, but having a plan will set you up for success.

CREATE YOUR BRAND

Once you are very clear on who you are and what kind of job would be your best job ever, you are ready to create

your own brand. We apply the term "brand" to products or services. We can conjure up a wealth of information just by seeing a particular logo. Think of the Nike "swoosh". It is simple, memorable and powerful. Brand recognition conveys an experience or relationship with the products or services.

Your personal brand will be the impression that you leave in the minds of the people you meet. The goal is to communicate:

- **Who you are**
- **What you do**
- **What you want to do**

Your brand statement should answer the question "Why should I hire you?" The goal is to create a short, clear statement that is believable, meaningful, and memorable. Here are some examples.

> I am courageous in the face of change and can put my ideas into action, igniting passion and excitement in the organization.

> My values are reliability and consistency, which may ensure there are no unexpected surprises.

> I am an Operations Expert. I strive to meet deadlines with certainty and efficiency.

> My passion is creating new products or services.

> I add value by creating and maintaining relationships critical to the organization.

35

Based on these examples, create a first draft of your brand statement. Then try it out on friends, family and colleagues. Ask them, does this sound like me? You may be surprised at their answers, and may need to ponder them for a while. Refine your statement if necessary, and then memorize it. You've now created your own personal brand! Easy, wasn't it?

Once you are completely satisfied with your brand statement, there is one more step before you are ready to go.

Before you Start, Google Yourself!

It is imperative that you know what your Internet presence is and whether or not it is consistent with your brand statement. Employers often Google prospective candidates. If there is anything embarrassing or controversial in cyber space you may not be able to eliminate it, but you should be ready to discuss it if the topic arises. The last thing you want is to be blindsided.

Contrary to popular opinion, you **can** change cyber space. For example I have a friend who was identified on a literary web site as a lesbian. As she was applying for a job in a conservative profession, she decided this was information she would prefer to impart herself, rather than have a prospective employer discover it first. So she contacted the web site owner personally, and explained that she was concerned that the reference could expose her to discrimination. The owner agreed to remove her name. This will not always be possible, but it is always worth a try. Bear in mind that it may take several days for Google to "forget" you.

What Type of Organization is Right for You?

A lucky few of us can translate their hobbies into fulfilling careers, however most of us cannot. This doesn't mean that we can't incorporate **some** of our passions into our job choices. If you enjoy children, maybe this means working in child-focused industries, or service organizations. You may not interact directly with children in such a job, but you will be making a difference to children's lives.

Organizational Culture

The *Oxford Dictionary* defines culture as:

> "the behaviors and beliefs characteristic of a particular social, ethnic, or age group: the youth culture; the drug culture".

Culture matters, and you need to pay close attention. It is often overlooked by both employers and candidates. It has often been said that people don't leave their jobs, they leave their managers (and sometimes team-mates). However, **people also leave cultures that don't fit**.

Culture is neither a negative nor a positive; it evolves with people and their environment. Outside of employment you can choose to belong, not belong, or be indifferent. However, this choice does not extend to our jobs. **We need to belong at least enough so that we can feel that we "fit."** If you don't achieve a reasonable fit in the organization it is hard to build credibility, perform as a responsible team member, be heard, or have your ideas taken seriously. It is also close to impossible to be happy if you are not a reasonably good fit.

The cultures of social groups tend to reflect the values of the majority of its members – at least in modern times. However, this is not necessarily so in business cultures. **A company environment is more likely to be shaped by the most influential people in the company.** Sometimes this is the senior management or CEO, but not always.

I have worked in some organizations where there were numerous changes in the senior executive. In one company this led to the creation of what I call a "shadow leadership". These shadow leaders were very good at what they did, liked and respected one another, and most importantly had the respect of their co-workers. Their power did not come from their position in the organization but from their positive intentions, values and work ethic. This group had weathered many changes of direction over the years. They kept their heads down and carried on doing the right things regardless of the now dysfunctional leadership. Needless to say, without their buy-in no new leadership was going to succeed. To this day, I'm not sure how many leaders and managers at that company were aware of their existence – but there is no doubt that they were quietly defining the company's culture.

Knowing who is shaping your company's culture can give you valuable insights into your company, and into your chances of fitting in. However, it is also critical to have **realistic expectations**.

> For example, Jack, a young marketing executive, decided to leave his existing job in a large company because he wanted to expand his responsibility for marketing and sales. Jack had enjoyed tremendous success in his career thus far but felt that he hadn't managed to stand out from

his colleagues. He wanted to achieve personal, recognizable success. He joined a smaller company reporting directly to the owner and was excited to be able to personally steer the success of the company. The owner was very impressed with Jack's experience and bragged to colleagues about his new executive. Initially, Jack was very successful. As he had in the past, he worked with outside consultants to create a new long-term sales and marketing strategy. This new strategy energized the sales team and there was an initial increase in sales. Because sales were increasing the owner was also happy, despite the high cost of the consultants.

However, the sales started to slow down, and the owner became disenchanted. He started meeting with Jack every day to pressure him about the daily sales results. He expected Jack to have answers to resolve the problem. He was astonished when Jack suggested that they re-engage the consultants to analyse the results and develop another strategy. The owner was reluctant to spend more money and advised Jack that he needed to develop his own plans. Jack experienced many physical ailments due to the unrelenting stress of the daily meetings. He began dreading coming into the office. He eventually left the organization and returned to a larger company.

Clearly the owner and Jack were in alignment on the goal

of building the company's sales; however they were divergent on how those results were to be achieved. The owner was so excited to hire an executive with Jack's experience that he didn't question whether his skills were a fit for his company. Conversely, Jack did not take the time to consider the limitations of working for a smaller company, especially budget limitations.

He moved into a culture that was not a good fit, with disastrous results.

> On the other hand, Christabel has been
> extremely happy in her job for almost ten
> years. There has been very little variation in
> her position in that time. Christabel works with
> the same software and the same customers
> constantly; and she completes the same tasks
> daily, weekly and monthly to achieve her goals.
> She is very good at her job and has twice
> turned down promotions. She likes a job that
> is predictable and values being able to set her
> own hours around her children's activities. The
> position she fills is critical to the company and
> the stability she has brought to her position has
> been appreciated and rewarded. This job enables
> her to excel in her career and meet the demands
> of sports and other activities.

A Good Fit is the Key to your Best Job Ever

Once you've figured out who you are and where you want to work, it's time to figure out how to find your best job ever. But as we've just seen, it's crucial not to overlook the

40

issue of fit. Whether you are a manager considering who to promote in your department, or an employee hoping for a promotion, fit is key. **Ignoring or downplaying fit is the most common mistake made in many organizations**.

People are often promoted based on their current success and skill set, such as Lou (the Sales Manager I introduced earlier). However, little thought is given to the skills and talents required in the new position. Conversely, sometimes we accept promotions for the wrong reasons. You may be motivated to consider supervisor, management or other leadership positions, but unless you are a good fit for management, it may cause more harm than good.

> James was extremely happy working at his job. He had good benefits, and his job was just challenging enough to allow for the many creative activities that he enjoyed in his spare time. His only dissatisfaction with the position was the compensation. At the urging of his manager and due to his desire for a salary increase he accepted a promotion. In his new position, he had ten direct reports, days that were packed with meetings, and exposure to a whole new political game that he didn't even know existed before he took the promotion. His team loves working for him and he has received excellent performance evaluations, but he is not happy. His workload has increased so much he is forced to work many hours of overtime, without pay, now that he is a manager. He has been unable to pursue his creative activities and is experiencing many stress-related health problems. James was unhappy

because he forgot that what truly motivated him was not money.

Sometimes our ambitions get the better of us:

A researcher I knew excelled at the creation of new products. Joan was happiest in her laboratory mixing and measuring, or with other scientific colleagues speaking a language that few in the organization understood. She was well liked by the staff. As the organization grew managers were needed and Joan was tagged to advance. When she was offered a management position she could not resist the prestige of the title and the money that went along with the job. But she was a scientist, not a manager. She had a strong work ethic and relied almost exclusively on her own competence. She needed to maintain control and didn't delegate to her supervisors, or ask for help when she became overwhelmed, which was often. By not delegating she became a bottleneck in the organization. This became a vicious cycle and she continued to fall further behind and suffered from physical and stress-related ailments. Joan eventually lost the support of her team because they believed that they were not valued or trusted, and lost the respect of her fellow managers because she didn't deliver to deadlines. If Joan had spent some time figuring out who she was and where she wanted to go in her career she would have approached this situation differently.

If she had figured out that her passion was for the creative process of product development, she probably should have declined the promotion. If she nonetheless aspired to be a leader and accepted the promotion, she should at least have gone in with an awareness that the skills required to be successful were far different than the skills that made her an excellent scientist.

Companies have very different jobs, which require different types of people. The key for both you and your employer is to find the correct mix. Think of James, who was extremely happy in his job until he accepted a promotion. In hindsight I'm sure he would have made a different decision. If you are driven to achieve and advance you need to find not only the right opportunity, but the right culture to support you. It's no use wanting your boss's job if she has no intention of moving on. It's no use joining an established sedentary company if you are looking for growth and challenge. It's no use entering a world of blistering company politics unless you are good at politics and enjoy them – otherwise, you might be wiser to stay out of the fray! If you do not like surprises or constantly shifting priorities then you would be extremely unhappy at a young or start-up venture where routine is non-existent and people may be required to wear many hats.

The bottom line is to know who you are and what you like, and evaluate new companies and positions of the basis of whether you will fit in and be doing what you actually want to do.

STEP 2: LAY THE GROUNDWORK FOR YOUR BEST JOB EVER

PREPARE YOURSELF

By now you have prepared your brand statement, which will be your guide to what jobs you will target and what you have to offer your potential employers. Now you need to polish your presentation.

Get your Wardrobe Ready

Don't ignore how you dress. It's all about making a positive impression. Whether you are going to an interview, a networking event or a social event, you never know who you will meet. **Always be dressed for the position you want.** That doesn't mean running around in a suit all the time, but making choices that allow you to make the correct connection with the people you meet.

How you dress is an important communication tool and should support your brand statement. Pay attention to the details. Research how the successful people in your chosen markets or industries are dressed and use this as your starting point. Of course you don't need to exactly match their style, but make sure that your look is complementary and distinctive.

The Internet is full of images and videos that can help you develop a style statement.

> When I was an accounting student I worked with no less than six colleagues, all competing for work within the firm. I noticed that one woman, with no more education than I had, was able to get more plum assignments and more outside work than I was. She was no more capable than I, so why was this happening? I started to notice that she always wore suits, stockings and heels to the office. I was a young working mother and didn't pay as much attention to my looks. I decided to change my appearance to see if it made a difference. It took some time, but I also started getting better assignments. Eventually I was able to work solely for the senior partner of the firm and was recognized as one of the rising stars. Of course, this wasn't all due to my wardrobe, but dressing for the part didn't hurt.

If budget is a concern, and it was back when I was a student, there are many ways to reduce the costs. You don't have to spend a lot of money to have a solid professional wardrobe. I found one or two local designers that offered free fashion consultants on staff. They consulted with me on my needs and selected appropriate clothing for me. I got great advice and my clothes actually cost me less than shopping at department stores. If fashion scares you, find an advisor. This advice applies to men too!

Prepare your "Elevator Speeches"

We live in a sound bite world, like it or not, so be prepared at all times to **succinctly** answer the three most important questions that will come up in social gatherings, networking or industry events, or more importantly, in interviews.

Create three "elevator speeches" which should take a minute or less each to deliver. Writing these speeches down can help you remember, but don't script and memorize these speeches. Just commit key points to memory and practice your delivery. You want to sound as relaxed and natural as possible.

Tell me about yourself. Your **Career Overview Speech** should include your current position, your years of experience, the types of industries and selected names of companies, key strengths and abilities; and conclude with your unique values and talents.

> **Mike's example answer:** I have been a senior editor with Timebomb Corporation for five years, where I oversee the creation of training manuals for English Second Language (ESL) in a variety of industries. Prior to joining Timebomb I worked for ten years at the University of the Yellow Brick Road, creating ESL textbooks for elementary students. I have a Masters of English. I am also a very talented writer and I specialize in making complex topics accessible and easy to understand.

Why did you leave your last job? Your **Leaving Speech** is critical and should be prepared with care. It can be a difficult topic to discuss, but if you have a reason that is easy to understand, and can talk about it comfortably, you will be able to dispel any negativity. Sometimes you may be able to vet this story with your former employer, but if not, make sure that you are honest but positive. Don't forget one of the golden rules of job searches: never, never, never belittle your previous boss and company (not before you have the new job, anyway!)

> **Mike's example answer:** When I joined
> Timebomb Corporation the field of training for
> ESL workers was relatively new and that allowed
> me a lot of creativity in designing the courses.
> Now that the industry is maturing most of the
> existing courses are only being updated
> as required, with less and less new projects
> coming in.

Now what? Your **What's Next Speech** should follow closely after your *Leaving Speech*. You will need to develop a few different scenarios for the type of event you are attending. You can speak generally about your skills, style, knowledge and where and how you hope to contribute. If you have more precise information in a particular setting you can tailor your general speech to specifically highlight the abilities you believe will be of interest to your listener.

Your goal here is to sell yourself, but don't oversell! Be sensitive to your listener's responses and body language. Are they staring off into space? Not good. Are they making eye contact and nodding as you speak? Very good. Stay attentive and make adjustments if necessary.

Mike's example answer: Apart from my writing and editorial skills, I am also an experienced desktop publisher and am currently studying web design. I have created four websites, including my own. I am interested in opportunities to use my writing and communication talents to assist corporations to create compelling web experiences that allow them to interact with their customers.

STEP 3: PREPARE YOUR DOCUMENTS FOR YOUR BEST JOB EVER

Ensure that all your documents are clear and consistent. Remember, these are selling tools. Consider the image you wish to portray and ensure that the message is communicated in the quality of all your materials.

YOUR INTRODUCTION CARDS

Your first step is to create an introduction card. This should include all your personal contact information, degrees or designations, etc. Make sure you always have a supply of cards, just in case you meet someone unexpectedly. You never know! You don't want to be the person scrambling for a pen and a piece of paper if you meet someone interesting.

Your card doesn't have to be anything fancy, but it should be polished and professional looking. The easier you make it for people to reach you, the better. (Don't put your phone number in a tiny, unreadable font – even if it looks cool!)

YOUR RESUME

Now that you have some focus you should be able to refine your resume to suit the position you are seeking. Don't ever lie, and don't tell your whole history. Leave something for the interview. Resumes and their formats have been covered over and over again, so I will offer only a few key suggestions.

Don't use Empty Words in your Resume

It can be tempting to use impressive phrases or the latest buzzwords, but all too often these are just meaningless words. Words that are overused lose all their value. Remember when "quality" meant something was superior? These days if you have to use the word quality, then it is often assumed that there is no quality at all. These days words like "creative", "motivated", and "problem solving" are so over used that they are rapidly becoming meaningless. So don't be afraid to use common language. It's best to use **example accomplishments** in your resume, rather than trying to impress with a string of meaningless buzzwords.

Correct Length for Your Resume

Keep your resume to **two pages or less**. Be succinct and make every word count. Unless this is your first job, there is no reason to describe every position you have had since high school. I prefer the use of "Relevant Employment History" or "Selected Career Highlights" rather than a complete memory dump. Not only that, no one will read it. For those of us with decades of working experience, less is more. I recommend that you document up to fifteen years of experience.

Make Sure you Lead with Your Strengths

Use the **top half of the front page** of your resume wisely. This will be the first thing an employer, recruiter or human resources professional will scan before deciding whether to read on. Make sure that you address the key criteria of the position you are applying for, so that you are certain to make the first cut.

Your Cover Letter

Again, make these **short and sweet**. No more than one page, and get to the point right away. What makes you an ideal candidate for the position? Mirror the wording used in the posting and be specific.

Make sure that you address it to the correct person, use the correct job title and state the source of the posting.

Lastly, I know that it is easy to re-use cover letters, but be especially careful. It's all too easy to leave in information that is irrelevant to the position you are applying to – or even phrases that make it obvious that this is a recycled letter. I've made this mistake and truly wanted to kick myself. Needless to say, I didn't get even a reply to the submission. For the sake of saving a few minutes on my cover letter, I wasted the hours I put into researching the company and compiling an appropriate resume.

Spelling and Grammar in your Documents

Please, please, please have someone you trust **proofread** all your documents. There is nothing more unprofessional than spelling and grammar mistakes. It makes you look sloppy, and dramatically decreases your chances of getting an interview.

References

As you are compiling your documents think about who your references will be. You will need at least one or two past supervisor endorsements. The best way to identify references is to call and ask if you can use their names, and have a discussion about what they would offer up about working with you in the past. Will they whole-heartedly support you? Can you anticipate any issues they will raise to a prospective employer? If you are trying to keep your job search a secret you will have to rely on their discretion, but if you are uncertain about this perhaps you should reconsider them.

> Employers will also seek covert references and will also check social media sites.

Don't be naive. The grapevine is a two-way street. You are using your connections to find the best employers and they are using their connections to find the best employees. When reviewing resumes I always look for connections that I can call for a candid discussion.

STEP 4: RESEARCH TO TRACK DOWN YOUR BEST JOB EVER

FINDING THE RIGHT COMPANIES

There are numerous resources online or at your local library to start your research. In addition to sites such as Google, LinkedIn and corporate websites, there are other lesser-known websites that are extremely useful:

On the Industry Canada website (www.strategis.ic.gc.ca) there is a central database of Canadian businesses. Click on "Canadian Company Capabilities" to begin. You can also use this site as a launch site to take you to selected associations online and to find the names of local member companies.

- CanadianCareers.com (www.canadiancareers.com) offers links to training, detailed job descriptions and questionnaires.
- FPInfomart (www.fpinfomart.ca) offers corporate information on all publicly-traded companies.
- SEDAR (Canadian) and EDGAR (American) (www.sedar.com and www.sec.gov/edgar.shtml) are government sites for gathering information such as annual reports. Annual reports are filed by companies each year summarizing their financial results, but they

also include management discussion and analysis, which can give you a lot of information about operations. It can be quite a plod to work through, but it might be quicker than navigating to each company website if you are researching more than one company.

- Newswire services or newspapers also allow you to access additional information. By using search engines on these sites you can review recent stories about your chosen organizations, including ones that the companies may not include on their corporate websites.

RESEARCH COMPENSATION

Sometimes our dream jobs just don't pay enough to meet our obligations. Yup, we have to work for a living, so money is an important consideration. Make sure that you research the range of pay for your chosen position. Defining your chosen position may not be easy. Spend some time reading the job descriptions in detail and in the context of the industries that you are targeting. Unfortunately defining a wide range of job descriptions is not standardized or scientific. When you are researching, pay special attention to years of experience, education requirements, supervisory responsibilities, etc. This may not be easy; compensation can be complicated, based on such general factors as:

- **Size of organization** – larger, more established companies usually offer higher salaries.

- **Volume of sales** – companies with higher sales volumes may offer higher salaries.
- **Specific industry norms** – salaries for the same jobs vary between industries: to give just one example, the pharmaceutical industry offers higher-paying positions than the natural vitamin and supplement companies.

Compensation and responsibility often go hand in hand, and in some cases the titles used in the pay ranks can be confusing. How does a "senior" differ from a "supervisor" position?

Also, education may impact your expectations. For example in some industries or companies having a Masters Degree or an MBA will allow you to command a higher salary. **Cautionary note**: Investigate this first if you are considering an advanced degree.

Salary Guides

The trick to getting the most accurate salary information is getting the title and the job responsibilities in alignment. There are many different salary guides, which provide a range of salary information based on standard job classifications. Here are some that are available on-line to assist you.

- Canadian Salary Data (www.erieri.ca) is a site geared more for employers than job searchers. It is a costly service, but has a free demo that can be quite useful. The demo will only give you a Canadian average, but it includes over 6,000 jobs and job descriptions.
- Once you identify the correct position title, then visit a few other sites (such as the three listed below) to

refine the salary information to your location.

- Monster (www.monster.ca – Career Advice), Wowjobs (www.wowjobs.ca/salary) and Payscale (www.payscale.com – Special Features) are all good sites to visit and compare information.
- Associations or recruiters also have published salary guide information, which is usually free.

Remember that the information you are gathering is a range, not a fixed number.

PUTTING IT ALL TOGETHER: WHAT DO YOU WANT?

Salary is only one part of the compensation package, and the compensation package is only part of your "Must Haves", and "Nice to Haves".

Before you go any further, create a list of the "Must Haves" and "Nice to Haves" so that you can make the most of your search. Consider the following items and add more if necessary:

1. **Compensation** – What level is acceptable? Would you be willing to accept higher compensation that came with more risk (such as with sales commissions), or do you prefer a safer but lower salary? What other types of compensation interest you – bonuses, stock options?
2. **Benefits** – Think about vacation time, health insurance, gym memberships, tuition reimbursement, employee assistance programs, coaching, etc.?
3. **Hours of work** – How many hours a week would

you prefer to work? Would you appreciate a flexible or fixed schedule? What about telecommuting opportunities?

4. **Length of commute** – Determine how far you are willing to commute for the right job. What types of commute are you comfortable with – transit, carpooling, car, bicycle?

5. **Advancement** – Are you satisfied with the job offered, or do you need a clear plan for advancement?

6. **Culture** – Think about the types of industries that attract you and what the cultures are like in those companies. What type of relationship do you wish to have with your boss and co-workers?

7. **Travel** – Do you enjoy business travel and meeting clients or customers? Do you prefer a position closer to home?

Add any other specific items to your list and then arrange it based on what is most important to you. This list will help you target companies, and may even guide **where** you look for work.

STEP 5: TARGET YOUR SEARCH FOR YOUR BEST JOB EVER

You should already have found some good information in your research on the Internet. If you are lucky, you will also have found some job postings that you can respond to. If not, you are going to have to be resourceful.

Now it's time to get specific and target the companies that you wish to work for. You should have some clues based on your brand statement. Then again, sometimes we just admire companies or their products. Either way your goal should be to find out if there is a fit for you, whatever organization you choose.

Make a list of your most important criteria and rate your chosen organizations. For example, location can be extremely important, as more people look to live in city centers without a car.

Other questions to consider are:

•   **Is the size of the company important?**

Most people know where they are most comfortable. Jobs in larger organizations tend to be more specialized and specific. This may appeal to people who like to specialize and be more narrowly focused. In smaller companies, you tend to have "hybrid" positions where there can be more multi-tasking required.

- **Is the type of service or product important to you?**

Do you need to connect emotionally or with pride to the company or its products? Not everyone does, or there would be no people working for tobacco companies or in casinos, but if you do care it would be best to make your list of "no-gos" before you start your search.

- **How many companies are in your target group?**

I frequently say that a job search is like being single. You have to kiss a lot of frogs before you meet your prince. Once you have a list of companies or industries that you would like to pursue, take some time to consider how many opportunities there are likely to be at any given time. The smaller the pool the harder it will be to find your job.

Once you have your short list of companies, then start to research using the various resources listed above. If the company is public then it will be easier to obtain information, if not then you may have to make some initial assumptions that you can refine later.

> When I had created my brand statement I
> realized that I could not earn a living at the
> expense of other people and the environment.
> As a result I decided that I could not work
> in the mining or gaming industries. I had
> worked in the mining industry in the past and
> could have networked to discover another

opportunity. However, I decided to focus my efforts elsewhere. The next week, I was called about a position in a gaming company, which I turned down. In the past my ambition might have got the better of me and I would have gone through the interviews just to see if I would get shortlisted. This would have wasted a lot time for something that would not make me happy.

Everyone is busy these days, so use your time wisely and respect other people's time. The more time you spend researching the companies and industries of interest to you, the more focused your job search will be.

Once you have developed your short list, then a visit to their websites is the first step in your research. Pay attention to mission and vision statements, press releases, and items in the news. The company job postings can give you a lot of information about turn over, as can press releases for senior positions. The more information you can obtain about the key executives in the organization, the more information you can gather about the culture.

Find out as much as you can about senior management. Many executives post information about themselves online, on sites such as Facebook and LinkedIn. In addition, there are also many other interesting facts you can find on the Internet. Whether you are applying for an entry level, management or leadership position, you need to know the organization's values. A safe assumption that I have used is this:

What is important to the CEO is usually important to the company.

I once researched a CEO and discovered that he was the founder of a charity supporting an inner city elementary school breakfast program. Not only did this give me a lot of information about his values, I was able to see how his values fit the company's mission and vision statements. This gave me a lot of confidence about the organization. Also, it was a great conversation starter in the interview.

Another CEO posted a picture of himself scuba diving on his Facebook profile. As I am an avid diver, this was again valuable information to take into the interview. However, it also gave me a sense of activity and health in the organization. I was able to confirm these assumptions at a later interview. This was important to me as it fit with my personal values and lifestyle.

Still another CEO I researched was quoted in a magazine article stating that money was his sole motivator. Clearly our values did not align, and I knew I could not be happy working in his organization.

Everything you can find out will be helpful in determining whether a company stays on your list, or not; and will be helpful in landing the job, should you decide you want it. Once you have finalized your list, it's time to start making contact.

STEP 6: REACH OUT TO FIND YOUR BEST JOB EVER

It takes discipline and determination to find a job, but it doesn't have to be tedious. **Make your job search fun.** Make plans, set goals and document the journey. Keep track and follow up with those you have met. Note what events were positive, and what events were less than positive. Writing things down will not only help keep you on track but will also allow you to see the accomplishments you made.

How do you make connections to your chosen companies? Traditionally people email in unsolicited resumes, contact human resource directors and apply for entry-level jobs to get a foot in the door. There are much better ways.

PERSONAL NETWORKS

Start with your personal network. Reach out to friends and colleagues to see if someone can make an introduction to anyone currently working for your chosen companies. This approach can often be the most effective because of the personal touch. Some companies offer rewards to employees for successfully attracting candidates, but that really depends on the state of the job market, the industries you are targeting and the economy. Almost everyone has a story about themselves or someone they know who has found a new position through a friend.

It's a good idea to start with a telephone call and follow up with an email. This way you've made two touches and your colleague can easily forward your information electronically.

> Be careful when you are using email. Once an email is out of your hands it can become anyone's property. Make sure that you use email sparingly and professionally.

Recruiters

Recruiters can often be a valuable resource. Many of these firms are specialized or have dedicated departments to deal with specific industries, and almost all of their listings can be accessed online. It is unlikely that you will be able to meet with these individuals unless you are applying for a specific job. This may be a situation where your personal network can assist.

Once you have made a positive impression on a recruiter they will keep in touch as opportunities arise. You will need to have a good relationship with **more than one recruiter**. If one recruiter has placed you in a position they also have a relationship with that employer. This means that they will not be contacting you for other opportunities while you remain with that company.

ONLINE JOB SEARCHING

Using online job sites is extremely easy, but there are pros and cons to posting your resume on job sites. Recruiting experts suggest that you tailor resumes to each position. You cannot get away with this if you have a resume available to the public. There is also a risk that your boss may see your resume and have some questions.

Most job search sites have a job alert system. You can enter your job criteria into a search engine on the site and you will be sent an email when there is a job posting that fits your criteria.

INFORMATION SOURCES

You can also cast your net a little wider. You've already researched key executives on LinkedIn; now dig a little deeper and look for other connections. These may be not as familiar as your personal network, but still can provide you with valuable links. People often list degrees and associations on LinkedIn, which can provide you with other ways to find common ground.

NETWORKING

Networking events can be of value. Both companies and individuals are able to join Board of Trade or Chamber of Commerce groups. These groups offer a multitude of opportunities to meet and network with business professionals. Boards often offer specialty group meetings such as women, entrepreneur or technology groups and invite speakers or specialized speakers. These groups can be highly useful if you are trying to move into a new area of interest.

The Board of Trade that I joined paired me up with an existing member to make sure that I got the most out of the experience. He would call me up on a monthly basis to chat and make suggestions about upcoming events, and often offered to join me to help break the ice.

Tradeshows and Job Fairs

Tradeshows and job fairs are another obvious source, particularly if you are targeting a specific industry. Tradeshows are usually sales and promotion events, so this can also be an opportunity for you to find out more about the company's products or services. Best of all you might find some quiet time to ask the people working the show about their experiences with the company. You may even get a business card so that you can follow up later.

Professional or Trade Associations

Professional or trade associations can be another opportunity for you to build your network. Attend periodic events and talk to the people in your vicinity. You never know who you will meet. Also, look for speakers or presenters who may have access to companies of interest.

If you have a particular expertise, then perhaps

participating at an event, or making a presentation at a conference, will invite introductions. Being one of the presenters at a conference usually means you will meet the organizers and other presenters – all valuable opportunities for networking. There is a fair amount of work involved in putting together a good presentation, but it usually pays off. What's more, you may be able to recycle the same presentation for different conferences or venues.

VOLUNTEERING

Volunteering can also be a good way to connect with people who share your values. I mentioned earlier about the CEO who founded a charity. Volunteering for a charity can give you a starting point for a personal conversation that may not have been possible through traditional channels. You never know where these connections can lead. However, it is extremely important to be genuine. No one likes a phoney. So if you decide to go this route, it is important to find a charity that is important to you, based on your own personal values.

HIDDEN OPPORTUNITIES

Sometimes the best leads come from the most unlikely places.

> A software technician I know relocated to a new city and was having trouble finding a job. Max was working in an industry that used a

particularly well-known software package. Doing his due diligence and networking he came up with the idea of joining the software company as a sales representative. Max contacted the company and was given an interview. Both he and the sales manager determined that a sales career was not for him, but a connection was made. Max eventually persuaded one of the sales managers in the company to provide him with a list of his customers. Through this list Max successfully found a job, and works there to this day.

I once made a lateral career move without missing a day's work. I realized that my current job was no longer challenging me the way it had in the past. While still in my old position, I started networking more with peers in my industry group and deepening my relationships with key individuals. As a result, I received an email from one of my colleagues advising me of an opening in their company and asking if I knew of anyone who might be interested. You bet I did!

STEP 7: PREPARE FOR THE INTERVIEW FOR YOUR BEST JOB EVER

INTERVIEW STYLES

Interview styles have changed over the years. An experience-based interview will focus more on your skills, ability and employment history. A behavior-based interview will contain more open-ended questions asking you to describe specific experiences. I usually create a combination of both styles when I interview but use more of the behavioral style. I count on the resume and the references to confirm abilities. Behavioral interview questions usually sound like this: "Tell me about a time when ..." Or "Give me an example of ..." Unfortunately these interviews are harder to prepare for in advance, but if you Google "behavioral interview questions" there are pages and pages of sites to visit for examples.

In these interviews remember to listen carefully to the questions and answer succinctly. The interviewers are trying to get a sense of how you approach certain situations, how well you communicate and the results you have achieved.

The Secret Language of Job Postings

Pay close attention to words that are used in the job description and the interview, as they may have more meaning than you think. Much like using the same tired phrases on your resumes, companies use the same phrases over and over again in job listings. But what they actually mean can vary from employer to employer. Make note of the words and make sure that their meanings are actually explained during the interview. If not, then ask.

Here are the worst possible scenarios for some of the most common phrases:

- **"Fast-paced environment"** may mean overwhelming demands or constantly shifting priorities.
- **"Multi-tasking"** may mean simultaneously doing the job of two people (for one salary, of course).
- **"Attention to detail"** may mean that the work is repetitive and tedious. There may not be much decision-making or responsibility in the position.
- **"Good team player"** can mean that you will be picking up the slack for less productive team members. It can also mean you will be working long hours, so you better like the team!
- **"Flexible schedule"** – for what; evening and weekend work?
- **"Entry level position"** – code for low pay.
- **"Improvement of process"** may mean that their computer systems or processes are out of date or inefficient.
- **"Good people skills"** – because your supervisor doesn't have any?

- **"Self-starter"** usually means that there will be little or no training so you better be able to figure it out for yourself.
- **"Results-oriented"** may mean that they don't care how late or long you have to work. May go hand in hand with multi-tasking.
- **"Coordinator"** often means doing the job of a supervisor, but for less pay.
- **"Great opportunity to build your portfolio"** almost invariably means the pay is too low for the position. The company is hoping that you will work for something other than the pay.

Try to frame some of your questions to help you uncover exactly what this employer means. Asking for an example is always a good, non-judgemental way to get more information. Obviously you want to be diplomatic, but some of these statements go to the heart of the culture of the organization. You need to know what you may be getting into.

Make a list of the phrases that you need to explore in the interview and cross them off or make notes as their meaning is explained to you. If you reach the end of the interview without this clarification then you can ask questions such as the following:

- Please tell me what a typical day is like in this position.
- I see you have used the word "multi-tasking" in your job posting. What does that mean in this position?
- How long do people usually stay in this position?

Roger was interviewing for an accounting position with a well-respected company. They had a great product and a great reputation. He had met all three owners at separate interviews and they had made a good impression on each other. He had also met with their auditor to review the financial information and was told this was a great company with a bright future. When the offer was made he happily accepted. By the end of the first day he knew that he had made a big mistake and less than a year later he left the company. So what went wrong?

Firstly, Roger failed to reflect on why the owners conducted their interviews separately. Had he done so and perhaps asked a direct question he might have uncovered a very toxic power struggle between the partners. Two of the partners were competing for the position of CEO and the third partner was stuck between them trying to keep the peace. You can imagine the tension when all three had to meet in person.

Secondly, Roger failed to ask a critical question of the auditor. Was the company experiencing any cash flow problems, or having trouble meeting their obligations? On Roger's first day, the partners were struggling to make their bi-weekly payroll, which turned out to be a recurring problem every payday. He also became aware shortly after that the partners had made contractual obligations to third parties for over $5M without securing the necessary financing in advance.

71

Telephone Pre-screening

Most companies conduct telephone pre-screening interviews. Often Human Resource professionals or recruiters conduct these calls. While there may be many attributes that they are looking for depending on the position, they are always listening for good communication skills, use of language and how energetic your responses are. By the end of this call, if you have impressed the interviewer, they will usually schedule you for an interview.

Sometimes a pre-screening interview may be used by employers to establish whether or not they can afford you. If you are asked about your salary expectations then you can consider the call to have been a fishing expedition and you may or may not be invited to interview.

> You always want to win at this stage so you can get to the face-to-face meeting, but not at all costs. So if you are asked for your salary expectations, do not sell yourself short just to get an interview. **Either the company can afford to pay your bottom line, or they cannot.** If they cannot, then you would be wasting their time and yours to go to an interview.

Schedule the Interview

You got the call back! Of course you will be visiting the company's website, but also make sure that you continue to impress as a savvy candidate, by following these guidelines:

- Always, always, always take the **first interview time**

offered. If you don't you may not get a second chance.

- Ask who you will be meeting with and then make sure you search the Internet for any tidbits of information about this person that you can casually drop into your conversation.

- Ask how long the interview is going to take. This way you can make sure that you give the interviewers everything they need to know about you before time runs out.

Get to the Interview

Make sure you know the route to take, and take a practice run if necessary. Allow extra time and plan to show up at least ten to fifteen minutes early. If you are late this will be seen as a lack of respect for the interviewer's time.

Always take any necessary bathroom breaks before you reach the interview. I can't count how many times I have come to fetch a candidate only to have to wait in the reception area until they were done. The waiting time always shortened the interview time. Does this sound like a picky point? Maybe. But these days everyone is so busy that interviews are *crammed* into everyone's schedules. You want to make sure you have the maximum possible time to impress. You also don't want to start off on the wrong foot, with your interviewer feeling slightly irritable. Believe me, this all counts.

Waiting for the Interview

You've got fifteen minutes before your interview. What should you do? Start with the receptionist. Have a good chat with him or her if you can. (This is hard to do if you are in the bathroom!) You can glean a lot of information about the company from someone who interacts with everyone in the organization. Not only that, but when I recruit I often use a receptionist as the first point of contact for every candidate. I rate candidates' team skills based on whether they were unfriendly or uncommunicative towards my receptionist. Being friendly matters, whether you are applying for a senior, intermediate or a junior position.

Apart from making sure you create a positive impression, you should also be getting an impression of the organization. You should have your "antennae" up, trying to get a feel for the culture. Do people seem happy, or is the office too quiet? Take in your surroundings. Office location and furniture can give you some idea about the image that the company is trying to project. Obviously if the office is sub-standard or rundown that's not good.

If the surroundings are really over the top you may conclude that the pay grades might be too. Not necessarily so – the furniture may be leased, or the company may have blown the budget. However, a clean, professional office should assure you of good physical working conditions. Unless you have a good memory you may wish to take notes while you are waiting for your turn.

STEP 8: ACE THE INTERVIEW FOR YOUR BEST JOB EVER

The interview stage is somewhat like the beginning of a relationship. Each person is trying to put their best foot forward. Additionally, the interviewers are fatigued and have a deadline to fill a position. They are looking for someone to stand out. It's easy to let ambition overcome you and hear what you want to hear, not what is actually being said. Slow down and listen at least as much as you speak. This is a big decision and you want to find your fit, not win an interview contest.

You already know your own brand, and the kind of culture in which you can feel happy and thrive. Now **you need to see whether the company would fit your needs**, so the more information you can obtain in the interview the better. Obviously you will be asking and answering questions, but remember, you are both putting on a bit of a performance during the interview. So how can you get the most information?

Body language between your interviewers is a good place to start. Ask yourself:

- How do they behave towards one another? This will give you clues about the style of the organization. Does it seem casual or formal? Compare this with your preferred working environment.

- Where do they sit; close together or far apart? Try to determine whether they seem to genuinely enjoy working together or are merely tolerating one another. This will give you clues about the level of respect that is acceptable in the organization.
- Do they maintain eye contact with one you? If one of the interviewers breaks eye contact with you when the other interviewer is speaking this may be a sign that they are uncomfortable with what is being said.
- Who does most of the talking? This again goes to respect. If more than one interviewer is involved in the meeting there must be a reason. So if only one is monopolizing the conversation you may try to figure out if this is by design, with one person merely observing, or whether someone just likes the sound of their own voice. If this is your potential boss, decide whether you like the sound of their voice because you may be hearing it a lot.

I was once part of the interview process to hire a senior marketing executive. The company was on a rocky financial footing and the owner had hired a new CEO to work with our President to help us find investors. The senior management group did not know him yet.

For senior hires it was customary for the President to attend the final selection meetings. Much to our surprise the new CEO also decided to attend. We were not given prior notice, or his reasons for attending. Much to our surprise and dismay he wanted to lead the interviews.

We were all a little nervous because we didn't know what to expect. It quickly became very uncomfortable for our group because he did most of the talking during the interviews. More importantly he did not have much knowledge of the company or the position. A number of times one of us would need to add more information or try to correct some representations, to make sure that the candidate received accurate information. As we did not know our CEO very well we were quite tentative in our approach. Needless to say there was a lot of tension in that room.

We did meet an excellent candidate and we all agreed to present her with an offer. Imagine our surprise when she turned us down flat!

A few years later our paths crossed at an industry event and I asked her about her decision. She said that she could feel the tension in the room. She couldn't tell what was going on but decided to follow her instincts and reject our offer. That was our loss, and taught me a big lesson about projecting the right image when conducting interviews. The essential point to remember is that interviews are not only for evaluating the person applying for a position. They are a two-way street in which the applicant has the opportunity to assess the company.

Finally ...
- Desperation smells. Make sure that you are relaxed and confident at all times.
- Don't raise any dissatisfaction with your current position. When asked why you are looking for a job, remember your elevator speech – *What's Next*.
- Be honest. Don't try to anticipate what the interviewer wants to hear.
- Communicate your energy and enthusiasm in your body language.

Reverse Interview: How to Use the Interview as a Learning Opportunity

Too many people approach interviews as a one-way street. This can be like trying to insert your "square peg" self into a round hole. It is imperative that you ask as many pertinent questions as possible in the interview to ensure that you can make an informed decision about whether the company is right for you.

I suggest that you write down the "must have" answers for your reference before the interview. As the meeting progresses, you can cross them out or jot down some notes. These questions should help you decide whether this employer is a good fit for you.

Conducting a reverse interview will also depend on the style of interview. If the interview is conversational then you can usually lob your questions into the mix when a particular topic arises. If the interview is more formal then you should rather wait until invited to ask questions at the end of the session. If in doubt, ask the interviewers their preference before they start.

If you are going to start asking your questions at the end of the interview, make sure you ask how much time you have. This demonstrates that you respect their time. Also, you don't have to guess about how much time you have, and you can make sure you get the most important questions answered.

Don't ask mundane questions designed to illustrate that you have done some research on the company. Hopefully you've demonstrated knowledge of the company all the way through your interview. This is your time – make sure that you get as much information as you can.

Lastly …

> NEVER, ever use the reverse interview to ask about salary or benefits.

Questions you Should Ask at the Interview

• **Why is the position available?**

This is the most important question you can ask. You need to know whether this is a newly created position or a replacement. If newly created, why? Hopefully it is because of growth and/or success. If it's a replacement, then I usually follow up with "How long was the previous incumbent in the position"? and "Why are they leaving?" You need to know if the position is a revolving door. If it is, this is a very big red flag.

- **What is the key to success in this position?**

Be prepared to dig. Don't settle for a generic answer. You are really looking for confirmation that you have what it takes to excel. No use kidding yourself, or them for that matter.

- **What kind of people work best with you?**

This is similar to the "What is your management style?" question, which often is given a standard answer of "open door". By asking this in a different way you may get better information. By now you should have gained some sort of insight into the personality of your potential boss; outgoing or reserved, process or people driven. Now you want to determine if they value differences or prefer to hire people similar to themselves. Obviously there is no right or wrong way to manage people –you just need enough information to determine whether or not this is the right position for you. For example, if you want lots of feedback from your boss you certainly don't want to hear that he is "results oriented".

> George started a new job two years ago. He
> initially enjoyed his work, his co-workers and
> environment. He soon noticed that his boss
> spent most days behind closed doors and had
> not developed good relationships with any of
> his staff. George decided to take the initiative
> and formed a congenial business relationship,
> discovering along the way that his boss was
> rather shy. As one of the few people who spoke
> with his boss, George was eventually offered
> a promotion to a supervisory position. When

accepting the promotion George made the assumption that his boss was promoting him based on his excellent people and communication skills. However, he never checked this assumption with his boss. The reality was that he had been promoted because his boss wanted to mentor George in his own image. As you can imagine, this quickly became a toxic environment for George.

- **What was the best lesson you ever learned?**

This is quite an interesting question, which should give you some good insight. Everyone makes mistakes and a good boss will fess up. If he or she doesn't then there are only a couple of conclusions to draw. They could be one of those lucky creatures who have never lost at anything in their lives, or their ego won't permit them to admit a mistake. Either way this would get me thinking about whether or not this is someone I want to work with.

- **How long have you been with the company? What do you like about working here and what would you change?**

Listen carefully to how all three parts of this question are answered. The length of tenure of your boss can be a sign of turnover in the organization. Does the rest of the response sound genuine and honest, or does it seem like sales spin to get you in the door? If there is more than one interviewer in the room you could ask that person as well to see how the answers differ.

The reverse interview is tricky. Time is a factor. You don't get as much time grilling them as they get to grill you. You also have to make sure you ask good questions, but do not interrogate your interviewers.

- **Can I speak with one of your direct reports?**

This question is a big risk so you may want to ask it only when you have an offer. But they are asking you for references, so fair is fair. If someone absolutely refuses, that is a pretty big red flag. Then again, they are unlikely to give you a reference who will speak ill of them. However, you can at least gauge the level of candor or guardedness when you speak with that person – all will give you clues.

How to Close the Interview

Before the final handshake, make sure you know what the next steps are in the hiring process. The two worst mistakes people make in interviews is to ask too few questions and to **make assumptions** rather than **test their assumptions**.

> It is usually the questions that you don't ask that can result in unpleasant surprises on the job.

Ask the following questions:

- **What are the next steps?**

You want to know how much longer they will be conducting initial interviews, whether there will be second interviews and who will be conducting those interviews. If you get really lucky you may find out how many people they intend to invite to second interviews, which should give you an idea of the odds of getting the job if you get to that stage.

- **How will I be contacted?**

You definitely do not want to miss that call so be clear on how and when they will reach you.

- **Who will make contact?**

Make sure that you clearly understand who will be initiating contact.

- **When will they make contact?**

Be absolutely clear about the timing. You want to limit the amount of time that you will spend worrying about whether or not you are chosen.

STEP 9: FOLLOW UP FOR YOUR BEST JOB EVER

Make sure that you send a **thank you note** to your interviewers. These days an email is perfectly acceptable, although some people still prefer handwritten notes. The choice is yours. Make sure that you include some brief points about yourself and your suitability for the role they wish to fill. This will help keep you fresh in their minds as they decide.

It is also a good idea to follow up again, even if you are not the chosen candidate. This is a great opportunity to leave a professional, positive impression and shows that you are willing to go the extra mile. Almost all candidates know about the first follow up, but hardly anyone does the second. Why not? This is a great opportunity to sell yourself again and remain top of mind. The company may have other positions to fill, or your interviewer may pass your name along to their colleagues.

> One of my friends, Bob, did exactly this. He went through three rounds of interviews but finished second. He wrote to the employer wishing them luck with their new employee and let them know that he would still be extremely interested in joining the company if the opportunity presented itself.

As luck would have it, the candidate ended up resigning within six months and Bob was offered the job.

Step 10: Close the Deal for your Best Job Ever

You've made it – you are the chosen candidate! Now comes the negotiation of terms. **The most common mistake that people make is assuming that they cannot make any significant changes to an offer letter.** Again, this is the same philosophy as the reverse interview: the offer letter is a two-way street. Don't have your pen ready to sign until you've read the offer over at least a couple of times. Every clause is a negotiating point and you are a free agent until you sign the offer letter.

Review the Offer

You will already have created your prioritized list of "must haves" to be compared to the offer. Review all the terms in the offer and make a list of the terms you wish to negotiate.

Obviously the biggest concern is the salary, and it should be, but make sure you review the whole offer. Changing jobs is one of the easiest ways to get the biggest raises. Take your time and make sure you are being offered what you are worth. Remember also that every future increase will be calculated on this base. It never hurts to ask for more money, but be prepared to offer a sound business reason for the request, such as years of experience or specific skills you bring to the company.

> A colleague of mine was once able to convince a potential employer to increase their initial offer by 25%. This was possible because my colleague's unique skill set and experience which were much greater than the job required. Rather than being deterred by this the employer was able to see the extra benefit of having such a qualified person on their team.

Make sure that you have all the details. If something is not spelled out in detail then ask for more information. If the company offers a benefit plan, make sure you know what that benefit plan entails.

> Anne once accepted a part-time position, three days a week, expecting to have access to the full employee benefit program because that was stated in the employment agreement. Only after she started the job did she discover that she was only entitled to some benefits and needed to work four days a week to access full coverage. As Anne's husband was self-employed, benefits were very high on her list of "must-haves". If she had asked specifically what benefits she would be entitled to, she may have been able to negotiate before she signed the agreement. Never assume, always ask.

Compensatory Trade-offs

Approach this negotiation from a Win-Win perspective. You want to be happy and you want your new employer to be happy that they chose you. As you review the items consider possible acceptable outcomes. Be prepared to give a little. Be creative.

You may wish to have a lawyer or other trusted advisor review the offer. It's often useful to get a second opinion and to talk through your negotiating items.

Crafting a Respectful Response

Do your homework before responding to the offer. Double check your market information and make sure you can back up your salary request. Continuously communicate the skills and experience that you are bringing to the job. Most responses are made verbally, so practice your delivery and make your presentation as polished as you can.

To Sign or not to Sign

The process of negotiating the offer will give you valuable insight into the workings of the company. Pay close attention to how your concerns are addressed. Are you left with the impression that they truly wish to make you happy, or are they more concerned about fitting you into their mold? If at any time you start to have doubts, or your "gut" is telling you something isn't right – LISTEN.

Don't be afraid to walk away at any time.

I once was within hours of accepting an offer
and giving my employer notice when I said no.
I had sailed through three interviews with no
qualms, and beat out three strong candidates for
the job. Everything was positive. However, when
I countered a few items in the offer letter, all my
requests were categorically denied. There was
no room to negotiate and the reason I was given
was "that's the way we do it". Now the choice
was entirely mine. I could accept or not. One of
my "must haves" was creativity and flexibility.
It would not be possible for me to work with a
rigid corporate mindset. I declined the offer. My
decision was validated when I noticed that the
position remained vacant for quite some time.

The point is to make sure that you give yourself the best
start you can in your new position. This is a fresh start, a
chance to reinvent yourself. Don't settle for less than you
deserve, but remember you have to give a little too.

STEP 11: MAKE A GRACEFUL EXIT

The way that you leave your old job is as important as how you start a new one. You never know when you may have to deal with your old boss or co-workers in the future, and you will need them as references. Your first step should be to deliver your notice in person directly to your boss. Speak positively about your experience with the company, but give an honest reason for leaving.

If the reason is money, don't be surprised if you receive a counter offer to stay, particularly if you have some unique skills. However, counter offers are tricky.

Take some time to think about why you are leaving the company in the first place:

- **Why are you leaving** – specifically? Has anything really changed that now causes you to rethink your decision?
- **Is it worth it to stay?** There may be some lingering resentment that you held the company to ransom, which may make your future experiences unpleasant.
- **Why now?** It took you a long time to decide to leave the company and only minutes for them to make a counter offer. Do they really care?
- **Who will you disappoint if you don't take the new position?** If you have used a recruiter to find

your new position, they could believe that they have been used to enrich your current situation and will be unlikely to want to work with you again.

Once you are sure you are leaving, consider crafting a written "leaving message" jointly with your boss. This will keep you both you and your boss on the same page, and reduce the possibility of rumors and gossip. Again, be honest and respectful in this communication.

Finally, consider the people at your old job that you wish to remain in contact with. Reach out to them with a thank you note. Let them know how they helped you and how much you wish to return the favor. Make sure that they have your new contact information. You will have made some great additions to your network.

A gracious exit strengthens your reputation as a solid, dependable person with strong integrity. News travels fast in the world of business.

Step 12: Make a Fresh Start with your Best Job Ever

You are in your new job and you have an opportunity to reinvent yourself. You want to do things differently than you have before. Revisit your brand statement and revise your career plan. Ask yourself:

- What do you want to achieve in your new position?
- What new skills do you want to add?

Be deliberate in your choices and your actions. Pay attention. Track your accomplishments, no matter how small, and review them regularly against your plan. Consider keeping a journal that you can review periodically. Whether this is your ideal job or a step along the road, there are many ways to keep challenging yourself and continue to network.

1. **Start by interacting with your new team**. Listen more than you speak, and listen "actively" – make eye contact, ask clarifying questions, be engaged. Take this time to identify people who can help you, who can be your friends and who you may wish to avoid. Keep testing your assumptions, sometimes your initial impressions can be valid, sometimes they are not. Creating a favorable first impression is a critical step

in building your reputation in the new organization. If your first communication is problematic or negative you will have to work extremely hard to change those impressions.

2. **Avoid conflict and drama.** You don't want to fall into the cycle of gossip and judgements. This will start you off on a negative path that you may never get off.

3. **Be real and be honest.** Lack of courage will get you nowhere. The highest performing teams offer honest but respectful opinions to each other, even dissenting opinions. The surest way to mediocrity is to become a yes-person. Practice giving and receiving feedback in a professional way.

4. **Most employers offer tuition reimbursement** for work-related studies. Make a goal to maximize your training budgets every year. Not only will you be learning new skills, you will also be meeting new people and increasing your opportunities for advancement.

5. **Mentoring.** Many companies have realized the value of mentorship. Volunteer to be a mentor for a junior staffer and ask for a mentor of your own.

6. **Volunteering for projects** (including community projects) is a great way to enrich your experience. Not only does it get you noticed by senior management for going the extra mile, it is also an opportunity to showcase your skills and build relationships with different teams.

7. **Showcase your other skills.** Share your knowledge by speaking at training sessions, seminars or company events. Consider writing articles for the company newsletter, trade publications, etc.

93

**Don't wait for the next career crisis to hit.
Take control of your career.**

SUCCESS IS THE BEST REVENGE!

Want to show your old boss a thing or two? The best success is a life well lived! **Take control of the hiring process, find your best job, reduce your stress, live your values and achieve more job satisfaction.** Your new employer will also benefit by having a more engaged and productive you. As you are rewarded you will be motivated to improve ... a good cycle to repeat again and again!